SAULY BEE SAVES THE PLANET

PERMACULTURE STYLEE

SAULY BEE

CONTENTS

PERMACULTURE BOOK

Hey I'm Sauly bee and I'm obsessed with permaculture. Because I think it's the solution to all the worlds problems. And I just like doing permaculture stuff out in nature. It's somewhat nourishing for the soul.

I CAN'T DO IT ALONE.

I need everyone in this place to help me. In this world only 1% of the people are farmers. That means 99% are not farming. I don't see farming as a separate job for someone to have. I see it as something for everyone to contribute. Thus benefiting each individual and the whole. Just cos I like farming does not mean I want to slave away like a fool just to feed all your hungry mouths. You've got to bend to me too. Because I understand what it's like to be a farmer. I understand the soil. And I know it's not working properly. When I tell many people that I like permaculture. They will freak out inside themselves and subtly try and defend there lifestyles and thus trying to make me feel like my vision and passion is unrealistic. But I know that's wrong. Because I see no other solution beyond permaculture. I've been in the existential vortex of modern society. I'm not waiting for artificial intelligence to save us. Because all I see is technology is improving society for the elites. It's also creating plastic society's disconnect from the beauty of the earth we once had.

I refuse to make a compromise because from the perspective of the permaculturalist. The compromise is not fair.

My friends at granja tzikin. They have goats. They make goats milk products. They also use the goats to make compost and to be natural lawnmowers for wild areas. Although I'm vegan I'm willing to make a compromise with them. Because I feel they are being effective with the animals. In a holistic way. That's a compromise I will make.

I will not make a compromise by eating a cake at my grandmas birthday because it's a one off. Made with factory farmed milk and processed sugar. No. Because what if everyone like me ate cake at there nans birthday? Then my friend we would be perpetuating the status quo.

MY STORY.

So I was in a bit of a pickle after university. I'd been kicked out for being relentlessly unsuccessful in classes. I couldn't hold down a job. I was majorly regretting quitting my brothers band. I was feeling totally lost. I had no focus. I was dedicated to music but my spark was fading.

I sobered up. Spoke to psychologists. Joined a football team. Started trying more holistical things like meditation, yoga. Joined some bands. Found a job.

In other words I was healing myself. I even had a girlfriend at some point, that actually felt good. I was building my blocks. Once I sorted myself out I became more conscious of helping the planet. I somehow realized that the earth needed healing. I knew about global warming and plastic pollution. I was reading about the Green Party and about politics. How there was major inequality. In London you see the poverty, the pollution. I had awakened and I could really see what was wrong.

I knew that if I could change myself then I could change the world. But I was helpless. Veganism was a good educator. But permaculture was the game changer. My dream had come true. I was lead singer of a band, had a job I enjoyed and a gf. But I left it all suddenly to study permaculture.

Most people do a two week pdc. But this was not long enough for me. I went to Scotland and stayed with a forest gnome for two months. Studying and actively doing permaculture. This involved picking slugs off 7 different types of kale. I left Inspired but unconvinced. It felt like I was facing an immense uphill battle against the whole world. And I most definitely was. Even the people on my course wouldn't eat my delicious seven kale sourdough masterpiece. They just wanted crisps. When I arrived back in London. It was my cousins wedding. It was all fun and games but two hours in, I just shut down. I felt so out of place all of a sudden. Like where was all this going? I lay down on the sofa in my suit that I didn't want to wear and waited for someone to take me home.

I went to the local gardening community which was cute but not so epic as I had hoped for. However the head gardener recommended I go to a Jewish spiritual community in Connecticut. My mum backed me up on this because she was kind of obsessed that I find a Jewish girlfriend. And maybe the Jews would knock some sense into my unbearable existentialist crisis that could only be resolved by digging holes in the family garden. I had a great 3 months in Connecticut. Working hard. Moving bucket loads of food waste into compost piles. And doing organic gardening everyday. It was an epic mission. I had a cool American girlfriend too and made a song called 'living on a farm'. Yeah I smashed it. But to me. It wasn't quite enough. Back to the grocery in London for round 3. The grocery was definitely giving me hope. There my boss was helping me to understand that my vision was not delusional. How inequality and struggle really existed. I had many encounters with people in the grocery. I also met a bunch of people in a vegan cafe called inspiral. I was definitely learning and growing every minute. The battle was lost but the war was certainly not.

I left for portugal to really try permaculture. Rasta farm, kundalini farm, rainbow gathering, food forest and biodynamic Gypsy herb farm. All amazing experiences. But the struggle was not over. I was also grateful to witness my witchy girlfriend. So disciplined. Dedicated to massage, banging her drum, dancing in nature and gardening. Hippy style. Little did I know this lady was gonna be more than an inspiration and completely correct all the way along.

Back to London with new found fire. I powered my way into the winter. My job as an after-school teacher taught me that kids need to be left to relax and do what they want more often than not. With little pay and trudging home in the rain to save money for the bus I was going nowhere. So I wrote to a community in Israel. My friend had recommended it to me. It looked small. Like I would be vulnerable and exposed. Little did I know that it was small but huge and I would have many things to do everyday and many cool people to meet . Inspiring experiences for sure. I was up the tree picking dates. But critical mind was dissecting what was and was not permaculture. Although I was totally inspired, I was not fully satisfied. Strong, efficient, hard working community yes. Fully sustainable, no. That was what I was reaching for. Against all odds.

When you put your dream out to the universe it will help you. My dream required a lot of help and a lot of challenges.

I knew that I didn't want to go back to England. A girl recommended I go to Australia where I could find farm work easily. And she was right. Luckily my other cousin was getting married in Australia. So I ended up there and stayed in Australia. Grapes, weed, melons, blueberries, more cherries, peas, sweet potatoes, native edibles, more cherries. That was the order of farming jobs I had .Additionally a mini vacation to Bali with my girlfriend, which was more about healing my gut, fasting and all that. Although we managed to do some permaculture outside a water temple for about 1hour.

Anyway I hit Vietnam to do yoga because my back was messed up from the hard labor on the farms. Vietnam, permaculture- wise was not strong, however, I did do some litter picking on an island which was a great day out. I also had fun and released an album. The yoga was important. I was running out of cash so I quickly found a permaculture farm which happened to be in Thailand. Why not? Give it a shot.

I arrived with a friend. 6months later the government had me out of the country because of covid. But I'd truly learnt alot of tricks on this permaculture farm which included planting vertiver, making thermophilic compost, foraging salads from whatever the hell was growing and wading around in a rice field. I became so obsessed with growing food I stuck my bare hand in a pile of rabbit poo and got stung by a scorpion and still finished making my final compost pile before the sun went down. I was ready to go home.

The journey was not over. With England hit by covid. I followed my gf to a retreat centre in Mexico learning about connecting to the present and relaxing. But they also had me watering a lot of drought tolerant plants everyday. The plan was to go inwards. I tried my best but I also saved the watermelon seeds at lunch and sprinkled them outside my balcony.

Then I hit mazunte and that was a mad time. Meanwhile I didn't stop planting thingys in the hostel. Almost broke. The Argentinian invited me to landscaping job in Colorado. Now I'm landscaping in Colorado. 6months and I'm feeling good but also pissed off at all the rich people for making me do the opposite of permaculture 40hrs a week.

With a little money I began my Central America travels. Guadelajara For Lazer eye surgery, Chiapas for Mayan culture, nature and rainbow gathering. I then Jumped the border into Guatemala. I tried to have fun but kept permaculture as the main focus. I didn't want to be just another dude that tried to change the world but ended up having fun and trashing the planet. No. I couldn't do that to the people that had no hope and were being walked all over. Just to serve the rich. I cringed when I strolled past busy workers on building sites. Making status quo thingys. The jungle was inspiring. I met some cool people. Made a humanure compost and planted some magic beans. I also hung out with a herbalist lady who smoked all my weed immediately when I arrived. But it was fine cos I don't really smoke much.

Somehow I ended up at a permaculture village at the lake atitlan. And this is where my journey ended but also very much started.

COMPOSTING.

One day in Thailand I went with Nathalie to buy a shit load of cow manure. Little did I know this was the greatest gift. I was able to make a shit load of thermophylic compost. That was ready in two weeks. To make thermophylic compost you need a layer of poo then a layer of green material, then a layer of brown. I had the cow manure. And the green material was super accessible because the Uruguayans were obsessed with cleaning up the wild section with weed wackers, to make the land look pretty. So I just racked up all the green weeds. Then I mixed with a bunch of hay which was the brown and soon there was loads of amazing compost. I was so proud of myself when my first tomatoes started to appear. And the Malabar spinach came poking up. So yeah. Thermophylic composting is where it's at. You must read the humanure handbook. Making your own compost is the revolution. That's why I bought a t-shirt that says make compost not war. People find it endearing but I am totally convinced making your own soil is literally gonna stop wars from happening.

Because wars are mostly just about sharing resources. Monoculture farming has depleted soils so people need land to make food. That's probably why they are fighting over Ukraine because Ukraine has some of the most fertile land in the world. But if we learn to make our own soil. We can all have super fertile land. Plus with natural organic permaculture farming. We can create systems that continuously nourish the soil. Rather than continuously deplete the soil.

Thermophilic composting is key because it creates infinitely magical soil. It's actually quite a new concept because science has been able to prove and master it. Some people are a bit odd with making this compost. But I'd say don't let that make you feel disillusioned because you can make pretty good soil pretty easily. The only reason people are being so perfectionist about it is that there's so many hungry mouths to feed and no'one wants to help. So the farmers have to be really particular and efficient. But if everyone helped out. A diy compost would be empowering and also totally efficient.

NO DIG

So apparently tilling your soil is actually counter productive. I believe this to be so. Because it breaks up all the underground connections made by the mushrooms and worms. Then it compacts more easily after it initially seems more soft. Vital nutrients get lost. The key here is to prepare your soil without rocks or things that don't decompose quickly. Make the beds deep. Then just let it do it's thing. Keep adding on top layers of mulch and compost every now then. You can also have nitrogen fixers in your soil or things that re-nourish your soil. Flowers attracting beneficial insects etc. The nature will loosen the soil naturally and maintain it. So don't dig it up. Although it's a good idea to plant different things each year because certain nutrients might specifically be depleted. Although if you get good soil going it shouldn't be a problem. The nature will spread the nutrients and if you keep adding on top with compost your golden.

HE HEALTHY ONES.

One of the biggest problems is that the cities have taking the healthy ones. Then the healthy ones get caught up in all the unhealthy things and become trapped in addiction and suffering etc. we need to get these healthy ones on the permaculture farms. We need to empower them to natural build, make compost, grow there own food, save seed, preserve food, control water flow etc. I've seen too many healthy ones working in bars or in front of computers, building huge pointless buildings. We need to empower these people so that they can understand the vision before they got lost in the empty vortex of forever lostness and start freaking out. The system wants to lower the healthy ones vibrations so they can control them and enslave them as soon as possible. Before they realize that they can come whole and become one with the earth and the universe.

NATURAL BUILDING

Natural building is so so important. Empowering people to build there own homes is so important so that we are not at the mercy of these building companies who's underlying agenda is profit. I watched this documentary about earth houses and they were these genius diy earth ships that were thriving in the desert. Cooling in the heat. Warming in the cold. Made from recycled materials. The powers that be tried to crush this vision. It didn't fit with the status quo. Houses were supposed to have driveways. Have a porch. Have a connecting road. The demands were soul crushing. Crushing the joy of the ability to be creative and experimental. The main designer put up a good fight. He eventually lost. But when a natural disaster struck. He became the winner. Because his house designs were the best quick solution to repair the destruction caused by a tornado or whatever. Of course this was in America. But the world is overwhelmed right now with people afraid to step out of the box and try something innovative and new. Eco building is the most important thing right now. People need to wrap there heads around it. Especially the kids. The future generations. There are too many regulations on housing right now. Too many stupid rules are in place so the rich people can win. Eco houses. We all need eco houses made out of plastic rubbish and windows from recycled glass. Mud bricks etc. If people understand how to build in harmony with the earth the vision can change. Too many Andrew Tate like wierdos obsessed with flashing there cash and living in mansions. There's so many strong people out there that can make these crazy buildings like the gherkin in London. But if we were freed creatively and educated about natural building we could focus are energies effectively on future regenerative societies. What's with the idea that the strong men have to build everything. Our strong men are stolen by the rich. And they don't want medium strength people like me. In this community in Israel. Everyone contributed to the building of the penis palace. Men, women, young, old. All contributed in the best way possible. No competitive mindset. All inclusive, all welcoming society. That's what we need. So no one is falling by the wayside.

PIDGEON PEAS.

I am planting a million billion pidgeon pea trees and I will never stop because. They provide an abundance of protein full pees. So good food for humans. They also nitrogen fix so good for the soil. Chickens like them that can provide eggs and manure for the soil. So yeah. I'm not gonna stop planting them everywhere. And if you don't like peas. I guess your just being too picky and you don't understand that little trees like this are the kind of the things that are gonna save the planet.

FOOD FOREST

Creating food forests is the way. We can create a seven layered system where food is growing at different heights. Overstory trees, understory trees, shrubs, herbaceous layer, root layer, ground cover and climbers. All can mimic a forest system but provide food at the same time. This can be so easy to make abundant food. Especially if we are open minded about what we eat. We can literally create, with machines. A huge food forest by planting in patterns that will create these forests ready in 7years. This is called syntropic farming. Then you just give everyone a laminated sheet of everything you planted and they can just walk around and pick stuff and then drop it off In the community center.

MEDITATION IS KEY

Because we are just particles vibrating and in order to understand this we must meditate. Through meditation we can understand that peace is the key. Peace is what we are looking for. We can bring peace into our outer life. We can bring peace into our gardens. We can grow peacefully. We can build peacefully. We can make love peacefully. We can dream peacefully. We can eat peacefully. You catch my drift. That's why the universe is constantly hoping I stop drinking coffee all the time because it unnecessarily injects

me some adrenaline and then I'll manifest a confrontation or a fight with a polar bear. Most of the time this will happen in my mind. Like an argument about veganism. In my mind where a create a person to wind me up so I can get myself in a rage. At least I can acknowledge this. Coffee addiction is the debris of the society that I came from. These fast paced societies had me downing coffee just to stay focused and take me through the day. Thank you coffee. I now live amongst coffee trees and eat the fruit. A hardy drought tolerant perennial fruit tree. Heavily recommended to all you tropical mountain dwellers. That being said. My nervous system is way more relaxed than when I was younger. Will have to admit that coffee is my guilty pleasure. Sugar, alcohol, Tabacco. All dissipated into the abyss. But caffeine is the final frontier. Yoga helps me to reach a meditative state.

It prepares my body for meditation. It expands my lungs and oxygenates me. It activates my body parts and releases trapped energy. After yoga I can go deeper into the peace. Deeper into the love vortex. Deeper into the beautiful essence of existence we all most strive for. To crumble the ego, expand our consciousness and connect with who we truly came here to be. Which is.....

The thing?
We need to infuse this whole world with peace as quick as possible. Do a vipassana when you got a minute.

Jeff Lawton blew my mind when he talked about this. Basically if you spend enough time in nature. You begin to realize things. You begin to know just what to do. Just by observing you can see the patterns. Maybe you'll know exactly where to plant. You'll know exactly what to plant. We have this inherently within us. Permaculture experts say you should spend 1year just observing the land. For me. Just working the land, trying things. Whilst constantly connecting with intuition. Making mistakes and having some successes. But eventually coming out with a beautiful peace of you externally. Another thing is that we have spirit guides, ancestors and fairies guiding us. They will show you some seeds to plant, they will guide you to certain plants and flowers. If they think your up for doing permaculture. If you don't believe me don't worry. They will do it even if you don't believe them. Who knows maybe an ancestor guided you to this book. Haha. No escape from the Magic. There's a non fiction story called anastasia which i think might well be real. She is a magical being. Her idea of saving the planet is helping people who have committed themselves to little plots of land called daishes. There she can guide her committed workers. Anastasia may well be helping me on my peace of land because it's organic and no pesticide. I can't believe all the different things revealed to me since the beginning of my permaculture path. Definitely have a read of anastasia the ringing cedars of Russia and see what you think. There's literally people who have started daishes based on this book. . Anyway she can talk to animals and they are her loyal servants. Anyway next chapter.

SAVING SEEDS.

So why save seeds you ask? Great question. No1 it's a fun and meditative, an interesting earth connecting process. No2 you can have a second round of your food, herbs, flowers and you can have an exponential growth of food. No3 you won't have to buy more seeds. No need to spend money. No needs to bother the seed shops.

Things is the shops need money to pay rent. Thing is a seed shop should be a place to share and swap extra leftover seeds you don't need for the community. Thing is capitalism and all that means these big corporations have created seeds that do not create new seeds and are forcing us all to use them so we can buy them back from them and become dependent which has caused many farmers to commit suicide because they have been stretched beyond there limits. Other factors include dependency on machines and dependency on chemical fertilizer and herbicides. But maybe that's another chapter. The point is that we need to save the good seeds. The seeds that empower us. And make us more resilient for survival. The ones we can save and share and make our communities more abundant. No wonder the big corporations don't want us to know that because they want our money and energy. One time. My mum had a Tomato she bought from the shop. Her friends said she couldn't plant it because the seeds won't grow. Meaning they assumed it was a tomato that had been bred to not produce seeds that couldn't be replanted so we are dependent on the farms and can't easily grow our own tomatoes. My mother lady. She didn't listen and planted the tomatoes. The tomatoes grew! Victory against the Babylon. Nice one mom.

ON THIS BABYLON THING.

While we're at it. I'll tell you a story. I worked in a grocery. A family run grocery. Cos I was into permaculture and food miles and all that. I recommended to my boss that we sell locally grown food from allotments. He told me it was a way cool idea but the government had made it illegal. For real. Maybe the randomness of the food gave a certain health risk because lots of people growing food could not be monitored so easily. But really this example says it all on the tin. The government doesn't want to empower us. Doesn't trust us to create clean food and also they are most very probably encouraged by the big industry to favor there large scale produce over local organically grown produce.

Current food is done wrong for sure. Monoculture does not work. Did we talk about this? It depletes the land. Yes, the first few seasons it produces a lot of food but eventually the food quality is depleted by lower quality soil and chemical sprays. And then you get this fake food from the shops for cheap which we all love but it's all a con. We need biodiverse lands with variety and flowers. A monoculture farm can be destroyed in one day by bugs eating it. A diverse landscape will have one thingy gone but then the other will be fine because the bugs don't know about it. That's why we have kind of sacrificial crops in permaculture

I DON'T KNOW WHERE I'M GOING WITH THIS BOOK.

I don't really want to complain so much about the system so much. I want to empower you guys so that we can become sustainable and slowly dismantle the system by taking away its power. Oh yeah. And tell my story. Cos it's a journey now worth telling.

LET'S TALK ABOUT MUSHROOMS NEXT.

Basically mushrooms are generally underrated or overrated depending at what school your at. Mushrooms can heal, nourish and give a spiritual experience. I think foraging is a key skill we should all learn and encourage people to do more of. Finding mushrooms is a great day out and a good way to connect with nature. To enhance your senses as you search for mushrooms. Learning to identify these magical things. Mushrooms are one of the most healthy things to eat. Along with spirulina and other super foods. Which are many. One year the Chinese won the Olympics. And there secret was a particular mushroom which was giving all there athletes ridiculous health. That being said. Mushrooms is a great food source. In the community. The mushroom team, if not everyone can all go out for a day in the forest and bring back mushrooms for the rest of the week. I emphasize foraging. Why? Because I think this is the most green way of getting the food. Mushrooms are difficult to farm. They require a quite scientific process. In clean, controlled environments. Many people are passionate about this and can produce a load of mushrooms but is it on the base level a sustainable process? When we have to bring in technology we have to be careful. Technology requires energy. Technology might create plastics or waste products. Is it worth integrating a mechanistic system into a community for the long run? If every community was to farm mushrooms would it be a detriment or beneficial for the planet? I know that foraging may produce less mushrooms initially. Although the whole experience of gathering the mushrooms is far more nourishing and of course empowering. Anyone can forage. Only scientists can farm. If you get lost in the forest you can survive on foraging. You may stumble on a mushroom but you won't just stumble upon all the tools for a mushroom farm hanging from a tree. Like a fridge. Also if mushroom consumption became like a special thing rather than something we dump everyday on our pastas and stir frys then foraging would be quite adequate for our communities. Other food crops like amaranth would be the things we could always rely on to provide and mushrooms. Seasonally and sporadically. Infusing us with high vibrational nourishment every now and again.

TECHNOLOGY

Okay so I'm writing this book on my phone. So I can't deny the benefits of technology because when I sell this book I'm going to have one billion million. And then I can get mad seeds and throw them everywhere. I'm not anti-technology. But we definitely abuse technology somewhat. Humans are abused to make technology. Like child/ slave labor and all that. Digging for uranium or whatever. So is this phone ethical? Is it worth it? That being said. I've done the deed. Bought the phone. And so now it's time to ride the train. Hopefully there's some way we can make these jobs fairly paid and ethical. For certain. I hope this phone is made to last so not too many people have to suffer so I can have another phone when this breaks. Maybe I can put this phone to good use to enhance the lives of everyone. By encouraging a lifestyle that is abundant and joyful and doesn't require so much technology and therefore so much dependence on plundering the earth and crazy life threatening and difficult physical labor jobs. For instance we can create communities that don't need cars. People can just walk around. That is optimum. Technology has helped us but also crippled us in many different ways.

MEDICINE.

Medicine through herbalistical ways. Holistic ways should be encouraged in our new societies. Yoga, exercise, healthy food, herbal teas etc. these things will eliminate the need for money chemical warehouse factory based medicines. If we can heal ourselves we are empowered. By living well we can stop a lot of illness from emerging. Growing herbs and treating people holistically is also a more beautiful process. And don't require these strange sterile soul drying hospitals of the modern day. Yeah for sure. These places could be good in an emergency. But right now our societies are almost encouraging us to be ill with things like McDonalds actually existing. Once you understand nutrition. Places like these are somewhat preposterous. We can take our health back into our own hands. We need to activate and encourage the witches. And be healthy from the off. I know it's hard coming off from these sugar and salt filled Societies. But once you have been purged you will never want to go back. Or at least you will be very wary of the dirty traps poking out in every corner of the Babylon.

And you will be picking yarrow growing from the side of the road.

So yeah self healing, building the immune system, whim hoff. Challenging the body. Keeping the body flowing, spending time in nature and eating good fresh food. It's everyone's entitlement. Also singing in kirtan is some kind of beautiful vibrational raising activity. Especially mixed with cacao which is a super food.

SUPER FOODS.

There are so many super foods that are so very healthy that fall by the wayside because they are not normalized. Here in Guatemala we got. Chaya, amaranth, mulberry, Pidgeon pea and jocote fruit. That's enough to start with. These all grow super easily without much attention at all. So why not make them the staple diet? Simple maths. All over the world there is super foods sprouting out everywhere. Just leave your house and walk around. You may well have passed a super food on the way to the rainbow cash machine. Also eating is overrated. I reckon two healthy meals and then fasting past 6pm will have you buzzing. Not that I do that right now. I'm too caught up in the Babylon flow. But I'm not in my best health right now either. So. Yeah. Also drink plenty of water. Although all the waters these days are pretty polluted. But that's the fault of factory production and animal farming. Chemicals and animal waste leeching into the river. It's a Trash planet we are living in right now. The sign we return to Eden will be when the rivers flow clean. People in Scandinavia think they are so cool with their recycling system. They manage to recycle 80% waste. Wow! That means that 20% is not being recycled. Which is a hell of a lot of pollution. And they go around judging everyone else for not having proper recycling systems. When they are only successful by comparison to all the other trash guzzling nations. As far as I know. The only people that have zero plastic waste are the those that are living a more 'primitive' lifestyle. Those tribes in the amazon, Africa. Or wherever. Untouched by these modern psychopaths. Desperate to prove that Christmas is a way of life. And bicycles and cars are incredible discoveries. Modern societies generally do not have clean water. Untouched tribes do. Or villages up in the Mountains who have held on to there traditions. Don't worry I love you. Have a subway.

Anyway it's gonna be fine. Just let all that shit go. Relax unwind. Everything you ever dreamed will come flying in when you stop trying to force or serve your ego or anyone else's. You gotta tap into the deep space energy. The love energy. The universe has your back. The universe loves you and is willing to help you. Step out into the day and ask for guidance. Cry out to the lord for strength to persevere to the other side of the madness. To grow and flower. Like a flower. One love and peace for ever and everyone.

Ps.
I prefer using a scythe than a weedwacker because it's more peaceful.

www.ingramcontent.com/pod-product-compliance
Lightning Source LLC
Chambersburg PA
CBHW060347290526
45791CB00004B/1568

* 9 7 8 1 3 1 2 5 9 5 3 9 2 *